三条　陸・稲田浩司

Thanks for waiting, everyone!
Here is the first volume of *Beet!* Unlike
Dai's Adventure, which was set in a
world not too different from our own, for
this story we've constructed a new world
from scratch, setting up new rules for
the world, the Vandels and the monsters.
It's the biggest struggle we deal with, but
it also gives us pleasure to take on the
unpredictable. We'll continue to do our
best, so please cheer us on!
— Riku Sanjo

Author Riku Sanjo and artist Koji Inada were
both born in Tokyo in 1964. Sanjo began his
career writing a radio-controlled car manga
for the comic **Bonbon**. Inada debuted with
Kussotare Daze!! in **Weekly Shonen
Jump**. Sanjo and Inada first worked together
on the highly successful **Dragon Quest–Dai's
Big Adventure**. **Beet**, their latest collabora-
tion, debuted in **Monthly Shonen Jump**
in 2002 and was an immediate hit, inspiring
an action-packed video game and an animated
series on Japanese TV.

BEET THE VANDEL BUSTER
VOL. I
The SHONEN JUMP Graphic Novel Edition

STORY BY RIKU SANJO
ART BY KOJI INADA

English Adaptation/Shaenon K. Garrity
Translation/Naomi Kokubo
Touch-Up & Lettering/Mark McMurray
Graphics & Cover Design/Sean Lee
Editor/Richard Kadrey

Editor in Chief, Books/Alvin Lu
Editor in Chief, Magazines/Marc Weidenbaum
VP of Publishing Licensing/Rika Inouye
VP of Sales/Gonzalo Ferreyra
Sr. VP of Marketing/Liza Coppola
Publisher/Hyoe Narita

BOUKEN OH BEET – BEET THE VANDEL BUSTER –
© 2002 by Riku Sanjo, Koji Inada
All rights reserved. First published in Japan in 2002 by
SHUEISHA Inc., Tokyo. English translation rights in the
United States of America and Canada arranged by
SHUEISHA Inc. The stories, characters and incidents
mentioned in this publication are entirely fictional. No
portion of this book may be reproduced or transmitted
in any form or by any means without written permission
from the copyright holders.

Printed in the U.S.A.

Published by VIZ Media, LLC
P.O. Box 77064
San Francisco, CA 94107

SHONEN JUMP Graphic Novel Edition
10 9 8 7 6 5 4
First printing, September 2004
Fourth printing, June 2007

THE WORLD'S
MOST POPULAR MANGA
SHONEN JUMP
www.shonenjump.com

SHONEN JUMP GRAPHIC NOVEL

Beet
THE VANDEL BUSTER

Volume 1

Story by **Riku Sanjo**
Art by **Koji Inada**

THE VANDEL BUSTER

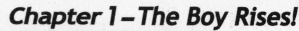

AS I'VE SAID TO YOU MANY TIMES, ONCE YOU'RE BRANDED, YOU CAN'T GO BACK TO A NORMAL CAREER.

...SURE YOU ABOUT THIS, REALLY... BEET..?

GCHAK

...OKAY WITH THAT?

YOU'RE...

VZ VZ

VZ

STARTING TODAY... I'M GONNA BE A VANDEL BUSTER!!!

TA-DA

ooo

GULP

I'VE ALREADY MADE UP MY MIND!!

ER... YUP! OF COURSE!

SHFF

Chapter 1 – The Boy Rises

BEET
THE VANDEL BUSTER

GYAAA AAAH!!!

N-NOT AT ALL!!

WASN'T IT PAINFUL? TAP

...WHAT'S HE DOING?

I'LL SHOW THEM... RIGHT NOW!!

AL-ALL RIGHT...!!

GAH!! THROB THROB THROB

...

NO WAY! I FEEL AS IF I'VE BECOME A GROWN MAN AND IT FEELS GREAT!!

VICTORY!!

9

THESE MONSTERS ARE NOTHING BUT THE EVIL SERVANTS THEY PRODUCE FOR FUN...

CRUSS

DON'T FEAR US JUST BECAUSE WE FINISHED AN EASY JOB LIKE THAT.

...

ALSIDE

OUR JOB IS TO DESTROY THOSE WHO CONTROL THE MONSTERS.

BLUEZAM

LAIO

THAT'S RIGHT. AFTER ALL...

...THE BUSTERS' TRUE ENEMIES...

...ARE THE VANDELS!

ZENON

Hidden in darkness, one day they appeared on the surface of the EARTH, multiplying monsters and destroying the peace and order of human society. Years have passed since that day.

Vandels!! In this story, that's what we call evil creatures with magical powers.

GOON

GO GO GO OON

...the Century of Darkness...

People call this seemingly endless era...

THANK YOU... THEY ALMOST BROKE THROUGH... THANK YOU...

NO PROBLEM AT ALL!

SHHK

HEE HEE... THE ONLY FRIENDLY LOCAL IS THE "GATE," HUH?

BUSINESS AS USUAL.

...

TH-THAT MEANS...

THEY'RE NOT THE KIND OF MONSTERS THAT COME INTO BEING NATURALLY.

THIRTY IRON RHINOS... THEY TRIED TO OPEN THE GATE.

H-HOW WAS IT, ZENON?

13

THE VANDEL BELTORZE...!!

HUBBUB

HUBBUB

S-SO HE'S COMING!!

THE "KING OF TRAGEDY" !!

THE RUMOR'S TRUE... HE'S NEARBY...

THAT POWERFUL VANDEL...

SHHF

I'M GONNA HELP YOU...

ZENON !!

THAT'S WHY WE'RE HERE!

MUTTER MUTTER

CHATTER

D-DO YOU THINK YOU CAN DEFEAT HIM...?

14

HE'S RIGHT. WE'RE PROFESSIONALS, GOT IT?

THAT'S ALL.

OUR JOB ISN'T CHILD'S PLAY.

WHAT?

GO HOME, BEET.

BUT WHY, ZENON?

I FINALLY MADE THE CONTRACT WITH VANDEL BUSTERS.

LOOK!!

GRP

THAT'S NOT AN ISSUE.

AS OF TODAY, I'M A PRO...

...THE REAL THING!!

16

YOU SAID THAT TO THE KID?

SO I MADE THE CONTRACT, DESPITE THE EXCRUCIATING PAIN!!

IT WAS YOU, LAIO, WHO SAID, "I CAN'T PLAY WITH YOU, KID. COME BACK ONCE YOU'RE A BUSTER." RIGHT?

Y-YOU... YOU...?

ER... I DIDN'T EXPECT HIM TO TAKE IT SERIOUSLY...

MAKE ME ONE OF THE ZENON WARRIORS NOW!!!

OKAY!!

LET ME JOIN YOU!

IDIOT!!

BA-CHAK

YOU...

...PO...

POALA...

HE'S A NEW KIND OF WEAPON, ALL RIGHT...

OOG...

ZHF
ZHF ZHF

OOO

OOO

OOO

I'M... HAVING...

...AN IMPORTANT CONVER- SATION...

THUD

I'D ALREADY MADE UP MY MIND TO BECOME A BUSTER SOMEDAY. SO WHAT'S THE DIFFERENCE?

...SHAD-DUP...

THRB THRB

WHAT'RE YOU THINKING? BINDING YOUR-SELF TO THE CONTRACT JUST LIKE THAT!

IDIOT!

IDIOT!

IDIOT!

...

HOW DO YOU THINK MY PARENTS WILL FEEL? THEY'VE LOOKED AFTER YOU SINCE YOUR PARENTS DIED.

BESIDES, ONCE I'M A TOP BUSTER, I'LL MARRY YOU!

I'M SURE YOUR PARENTS ARE GONNA LOVE IT.

IT'S ALL RIGHT. I PLAN TO BE THE STRONGEST, *THE FIRST-CLASS BUSTER* IN THE WORLD.

AS IF!!

WHO'D MARRY YOU?!

KA-POW

SO YOU'VE GOT NO WORRIES...

...RIGHT?

ALL RIGHT!

HMPH...

...WHY DOESN'T ANYONE BELIEVE ME?

I'LL EARN MY PROMOTION POINTS BY DEFEATING MONSTERS, ONE AFTER THE OTHER!

IS IT BECAUSE I'M STILL ONLY LEVEL 1?

I'M SURE I CAN RAISE MY LEVEL UP TO 10 IN NO TIME.

POWW

AFTER ALL, I'M "THE MAN WHO CAN FIGHT FOR THREE DAYS AND NIGHTS"!

SLLP

THAT'S RIGHT.

BEET IS A STRANGE CHILD.

HE SLEEPS ONLY ONCE EVERY THREE DAYS?

...?

IT'S ADVANTAGEOUS TO BE ABLE TO STAY ACTIVE FOR A LONG TIME WHEN PURSUING AN ENEMY OR GOING ON AN ADVENTURE...

HMPH. IN A WAY, THAT'S PERFECT FOR A BUSTER.

HE'S UP FOR THREE DAYS AND THEN SLEEPS FOR A WHOLE DAY... HE'S BEEN LIKE THAT FOR A LONG TIME. IT'S HOW HE'S BUILT, I GUESS.

WHEN ICICLE BATS PUT HOLES IN THE ROOF OF THE INN, HE FIXED IT IN THREE DAYS ON HIS OWN.

HE'D PLAY OR DO CHORES FOR THREE DAYS STRAIGHT.

IF A MONSTER ATTACKED HIM WHILE HE WAS ASLEEP, HE'D BE IN REAL TROUBLE.

RIGHT?

I'M NOT SO SURE! AFTER FIXING THAT ROOF, HE FELL ASLEEP WHILE HE WAS TAKING A BATH AND SLEPT THERE ALL DAY.

I MEANT TO RAISE THAT BOY TO LEAD A NORMAL LIFE, BUT...

I'M SORRY, ZENON.

...

...

BY THE TIME HE WOKE UP, HIS SKIN WAS TOTALLY WRINKLED.

LET ME CHECK UP ON HIM A BIT...

THUD

THANKS A LOT...

...LAIO.

IT'S THE LEAST I CAN DO.

YOU ALWAYS LET US STAY AT YOUR PLACE, EVERY TIME WE COME TO THE VILLAGE. IF YOU DIDN'T, WE'D HAVE TO CAMP OUT.

AH, BUT HOW TIRE-SOME...

...COULD IT MEAN HE HAS...

...THAT MUCH MORE POWER?

IF THIS BOY IS BORN WITH THE NEED TO SLEEP LONGER...

US BUSTERS HAVE FOUND THERE'S A STRONG LINK BETWEEN OUR ABILITIES AND OUR NEED FOR REST.

HEY!! LET GO! FIGHT ME FACE TO FACE!!

...

SPLOOSH!!

SPLOOSH SPLOOSH

GYAAAAH!!!

OU-OU-OUCH!!!

WHAM

WHAM

WHAM

DIDN'T I JUST TELL YOU? YOU CAN'T USE THE SPEAR LIKE THAT WHEN YOU ATTACK...

23

NEVER!! N-NO!!

IF YOU AGREE NOT TO BECOME ONE...

...I'LL HELP YOU OUT!

I'M TELLING YOU, YOU'RE BETTER OFF NOT BECOMING A BUSTER!!

HOW CAN— IT HURTS LIKE CRAZY!

BUT—

BUT—

...!

LOOSEN UP!

⁉

FWOOO

LOOSEN UP FIRST!

IF YOU TIGHTEN YOUR MUSCLES, THE TEETH WILL SINK FURTHER.

24

HOLD THE NECK OF THE SPEAR AND, USING THE POINT, CUT THE MOUTH OFF THE SHELL FROM BEHIND!

IT'S NOT AS PAINFUL AS BEFORE!!

AHH... HE'S RIGHT!

PLOP

SLICE

SU SU

IT'S THE FIRST TIME I EVER DEFEATED A MONSTER!

I-- I DID IT!!

I DID IT!!

YIPPEE!!

!!

SLOSH SLOSH SLOSH

25

YOU IDIOT! YOU GET THE FEWEST PROMOTION POINTS FROM THE BITING CLAMS!!

SO HOW MANY PROMOTION POINTS DO I GET FROM THIS ONE?

AM I UP TO LEVEL 5 OR SOMETHING LIKE THAT?

THANKS!

I DIDN'T EXPECT YOU TO GIVE ME ADVICE, ZENON!!

...

!

HUH

I'LL SURPRISE YOU BY GETTING STRONGER WHILE YOU GUYS ARE STILL IN THE VILLAGE!!

WELL, NONETHELESS, I'LL DO MY BEST!

...A LONGER ROAD THAN I EXPECTED, HUH?

...

YOU'LL BE LUCKY TO REACH LEVEL 3 EVEN AFTER YOU KILL OFF A HUNDRED OF THEM.

WHY DO YOU WANT TO BECOME A BUSTER SO MUCH?

IT'S BE-CAUSE...

WELL? HOW COME?

HUH?

...

BY "FIGHTING THREE DAYS AND NIGHTS," HUH?

YOU DON'T GIVE UP, DO YOU?

I WANNA BE A BUSTER LIKE THAT!!

YEAH! ZENON WARRIORS ARE THE BUSTERS OF JUSTICE, GETTING RID OF THE VANDELS AND PROTECTING HUMANS, RIGHT?

...I WANNA BE COOL LIKE YOU GUYS, ZENON!

...LIKE US?

YOU'VE SEEN THE WAY THE VILLAGERS LOOK AT US, HAVEN'T YOU? WE RISK OUR LIVES EVERY DAY, BUT NOBODY LIKES US.

YOU WON'T LAST LONG IDOLIZING THE JOB OR THINKING IT'S ALL FUN.

TO BE HONEST, IT'S NOT ALL THAT COOL.

JUSTICE... HOO BOY...

IT'S UNDER-STANDABLE.

ALTHOUGH OUR ENEMIES AREN'T HUMAN, WE AREN'T TOO DIFFERENT FROM ASSASSINS.

IN A WAY, WE'RE TREATED LIKE THE VANDELS.

BEET, KILLING VANDELS AND MONSTERS IS A BUSTER'S JOB. SIMPLE AS THAT.

OR DO YOU WANT TO BRAG ABOUT KILLING THE MONSTERS?

SO ARE YOU FIGHTING FOR MONEY?

THAT'S NOT TRUE!

WE CAN'T CALL... WHAT WE DO... JUSTICE.

...THAT'S TRUE, BUT...

YOU'RE WORKING HARD FOR THE SAKE OF THE VILLAGERS AND PEOPLE AROUND THE WORLD!!

I DON'T THINK SO!

THAT'S WHAT'S CALLED JUSTICE!!

DON'T YOU KNOW?

SHEEN

HIYAAH!!

ZENON...

...

I'M ALL PREPARED, SO WHY DON'T YOU GO BACK AND SLEEP.

OKAY! NOW THAT I KNOW WHAT TO DO, LET ME CLEAN UP THIS POND!!

...

I'VE GOT THIS FEELING HE'S REALLY GONNA CHANGE SOME-DAY...

THANKS TO ZENON'S ADVICE, I CAN EASILY DESTROY BITING CLAMS NOW!

HEE HEE HEE...

SPLASH

SPLASH

SLSSSS

GYAHH

NUTS!! I'M FADING...

BYAAAAAA

ONLY ONES LEFT ARE...

HUH...

HUH...

SPLASH

SPLASH

NO... SHOULDN'T... SLEEP HERE...

OH, YEAH... TODAY'S... MY DAY TO SLEEP...

DIZZY...

SPLASH

THEY'LL BITE ME... ALL OVER...

...

...HE'S COMING!

...!?

TMP

...YOU'RE...
!!

SMIRK

I SLEPT IN THE WATER ALL DAY AGAIN... THIS IS NOT GOOD.

SPLASH

BLOOP

BLOOP

...

RRUMBLE

CHK

36

THE VANDEL'S INCREDIBLE... BUT WHAT'RE THOSE THINGS? THOSE WEAPONS THEY'RE HOLDING?

AH! WOW!

NO OTHER BUSTER HAS CORNERED ME SO FAR...

NO VANDEL'S CORNERED ME.

CROWN SHIELD!

BURNING LANCE!

CYCLONE GUNNER!

38

IT'S USUALLY HIDDEN INSIDE THE BUSTER'S BODY. IT'S THE LAST WEAPON A BUSTER USES, UNSHEATHED ONLY IN TIMES OF GREAT DANGER...

A SAIGA IS A BUSTER'S STRONGEST DEFENSE.

SAIGA?

SAIGA!

THIS IS THE FIRST TIME WE'VE BROUGHT OUT ALL FIVE OF OUR SAIGA.

THE VILLAGE?

THIS IS IT, BELTORZE! WE WON'T LET YOU TOUCH THAT VILLAGE!!

SO A SAIGA... COMES RIGHT OUT OF THE BODY!?

!!?

I'M NOT INTERESTED IN THAT TO BEGIN WITH.

THE VILLAGE, INDEED...

HA HA HA... NOT A PROBLEM.

WH-WHAT!?

ALL I WANT IS YOUR FIVE HEADS.

ANY PLACE WOULD'VE BEEN FINE, SO LONG AS YOU WERE THERE!

WE VANDELS PUT A PRICE ON THE HEADS OF STRONG BUSTERS!

BY TAKING FIVE OF YOUR LIVES, I CAN GET ONE OF THESE.

I HEAR HUMANS DO THE SAME THING.

...HE'D FLATTEN THE VILLAGE!

F-FOR THAT LITTLE CHIP OF GLASS...

IT'S A STAR. DESTROYING A WHOLE COUNTRY WON'T EARN A SINGLE STAR.

ISN'T IT AN ECSTATIC MOMENT FOR A WARRIOR?

WHAT DO YOU THINK? ISN'T THAT TOUCHING TO LEARN THAT YOU'RE VALUED SO HIGHLY?

IN OTHER WORDS, YOUR DEATHS ARE WORTH MORE THAN AN ENTIRE COUNTRY.

GOT IT?

SNARL

BEL-TORZE... IT'S UNFOR-GIVABLE!!

WE'LL KILL YOU!!!

BEET SAW IT!!

THE DEATH MATCH...

...BETWEEN THE VANDEL AND THE BUSTERS, TWO SIDES AT THE HEIGHT OF THEIR POWERS.

44

IT'S AS IF THEY'RE IN ANOTHER WORLD!

T-TOO INCREDIBLE... NO WONDER THEY NEVER TOOK ME SERIOUSLY...

FOR BEET, LEVEL 1...

...IT LOOKED LIKE A MATCH AMONG THE GODS IN THE HEAVENS!!!

THEY'LL WIN!!

YES!! IT LOOKS LIKE ZENON'S TEAM IS STRONGER!

45

46

GSSSH

KA SHIK

HE'S TAKEN HIM HOSTAGE!!

GASP!

NO!!

GSH GSH

SMRK

HOSTAGE?

47

48

ZUGA

AAH

!!!

THTHTH THTHTH THD

50

GRRRRMBL

HAH

I WON!!

I HAD TO USE UP ALL THE DARK POWER I POSSESS... BUT I'M SURE I DEALT EACH OF THEM A FATAL BLOW!!

HAH

HAH

HAH

HAH

GASP—

TMP

THEY MAY THINK THEY COULD HIDE UNDER THE SMOKE, BUT THEY WON'T BE ABLE TO ESCAPE...

GRM

ALL I NEED TO DO IS TO FIND THEM AND TEAR OFF THEIR HEADS!

HUH— HUH— HUH—

KATCHUK

HOW'S... BEET?

WE'RE IN... REAL TROUBLE... THE WAY IT IS... WE'LL BE... ANNIHILATED...

...!!

DON'T TALK...

...BEET!!

GOOSH

S-SORRY... ZENON... IT'S... MY FAULT...

...YOU... COULD'VE... WON...

53

THAT'S RIGHT!! THERE'S... ONE WAY...

...

...!

BUT... CAN'T USE THAT...

NO TIME TO WASTE!

LET'S DO IT!

VROOM VMMM

ZENON! I READ YOUR MIND!

SHUFF

!!

BUT YOU'LL ALL—

WE'RE DYING... BUT IF WE POOL OUR ENERGY WITHIN SAIGA, WE CAN SAVE ONE LIFE...

...OF COURSE!

VMMMMM...

SHOO

SHUUU

YOU'VE SAVED EACH OF US AT LEAST ONCE BEFORE!

VUUUU...

NO NEED TO FEEL THAT WAY, ZENON!

WE'LL GATHER OUR LIFE FORCES. USE THEM AS YOU WISH!

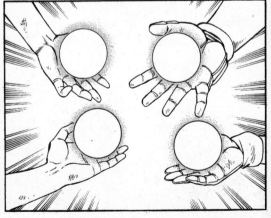

HEH ... I BELIEVE HE'S GONNA TRANSFORM SOMEDAY.

BE-SIDES... LIKE I TOLD YOU...

HE'S RIGHT... FOR THE SAKE OF THAT BOY'S BELIEFS...

...WE MUST NOT LET HIM DIE!!

DON'T YOU KNOW?

THAT'S WHAT'S CALLED JUSTICE!!

ALL OF YOU...

...THANKS!!

VUUUM...

...?

WE'RE GOING TO PUT ALL OF OUR REMAINING LIFE FORCE INSIDE OUR SAIGA AND INSERT THEM INTO YOUR BODY.

BEET, LISTEN CAREFULLY!

57

IF YOU DO THAT... YOU WON'T BE ABLE TO FIGHT ANY-MORE...

WHAT'RE YOU TALKING ABOUT...?

KOFF

WH...?

EVEN IF YOU'RE THE ONLY ONE...

...YOU MUST SURVIVE NO MATTER WHAT!!

A LEVEL 1 BUSTER SHOULDN'T HAVE TO LOOK AFTER US BIG BOYS.

DON'T WORRY ABOUT US!

KO FF KO FF

IF THAT GUY ATTACKS AGAIN...

KO FF

...FOR SOME-ONE LIKE ME...?

NO! DON'T! WHY... DO THAT...

DOON

UGH...

AAAAH...

SHAAAAA

READY...

...ALL THE TROUBLE!!

I-I CAUSED...

DON'T YOU UNDERSTAND? HAVE YOU EVER LOOKED AT YOURSELF IN THE MIRROR?

YOU IDIOT!

WHAT?

DON'T YOU THINK YOU RESEMBLE SOME- ONE?

YOUR EYES, YOUR MOUTH, YOUR WILD HAIR...

...IT'S NOT THE SAME WITH ZENON.

BUT...

...WE THOUGHT OF YOU AS IF YOU WERE OUR LITTLE BROTHER.

ALTHOUGH WE TRIED TO GIVE YOU THE COLD SHOULDER...

I HOPED... YOU COULD LEAD A LIFE WITHOUT VIOLENCE...

...ESPE- CIALLY IN THE ERA WE LIVE IN.

THAT'S WHY I LEFT YOU IN THIS VILLAGE WHEN YOU WERE A BABY.

...IT'S NOT "AS IF" FOR HIM.

...!!

ZENON'S MY...

NO WAY... ZENON'S...

61

I...

...WAIT... WAIT FOR ME...

SOME-DAY...

NO MATTER WHAT...

POALA...

ALL OF YOU...

I'M GLAD YOU'RE FINALLY AWAKE!

...!

WHERE'RE THE ZENON WARRIORS?

THEY'RE NOWHERE... AND THE VANDEL IS GONE.

DON'T KNOW...

64

I'M GONNA BECOME THE MAN WHO'LL GET RID OF ALL THE VANDELS AND END THE DARK AGE!

SOMEDAY, I'LL... I'LL BE AN INCREDIBLE BUSTER LIKE THE ZENON WARRIORS!

GRP

...!?

POALA...

...THAT I'LL CRY... SHAME-LESSLY... LIKE THIS...

THAT'S WHY... THIS IS THE LAST DAY...

...BEET...

UH UH UH UH...

UH... UH UH...

...

65

A PITY THE ZENON WARRIORS ARE GONE...

IF ONLY WE COULD HIRE A BUSTER TO HELP YOU OUT.

・・・

IF YOU'RE STILL ALIVE, HURRY UP AND COME BACK!

I'LL PROTECT THIS VILLAGE, ALL RIGHT?

...THERE'S NO POINT IN MOPING OVER THOSE WHO AREN'T HERE!

IDIOT!!

WHERE'VE YOU BEEN WANDERING AROUND FOR THREE YEARS, BEET?

GEEZ!

AREN'T YOU SUPPOSED TO BECOME AN INCREDIBLE BUSTER?

ARRGH

GRRR

DAAAA

oooooo

READ THIS WAY

I SLEPT A WHOLE DAY IN THE WATER AGAIN...

ARGH... TOO BAD...

HM?

OKAY!

RUB RUB RUB

KA-RA-CK

I HAVEN'T BEEN TRAINING FOR THREE YEARS FOR NOTH-ING...

HA HA HA! DON'T BITE ME! IF YOU DO, YOU'LL GET YOURSELF IN REAL TROUBLE!

69

Chapter 2:
He Who Returned

EEK!!

JUST BECAUSE THE "GATE" CANNOT SMELL, YOU MIGHT'VE THOUGHT YOU COULD FOOL US.

NO USE PRETENDING.

WH-WHAT'RE YOU DOING?

GONE MAD OR WHAT?

IT'S YOU, POALA!

...OR TAKING ADVANTAGE OF YOUR REACTION TO FLAME...

MONSTERS LIKE YOU CAN BE DESTROYED BY DAMAGING YOUR HEADS...

SHS S S

...THAT YOU'RE DRAW-MEN!

BUT IT'S EASY TO TELL FROM THAT OILY SMELL OF YOURS...

ooooo

ooooo

BA A

FIRE !!

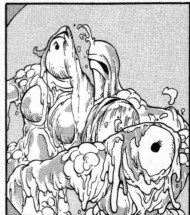

THE PROMOTION POINTS ARE 320...

CLANG

YOU'VE GOTTEN RID OF SOME PRETTY TOUGH ONES.

TWO BODIES OF DRAWMEN.

THIS UPS YOU TO LEVEL 21, POALA.

76

NEXT TIME, MAKE SURE YOU HAVE A MOUND OF MONEY READY!

ALL RIGHT, I'LL BE BACK SOON.

THANKS. ♪

YOUR COMMISSION.

HERE.

CHANK

YOU MEAN IT, DON'T YOU?

SHRP

MUGAIN
MG 85000

MUGAIN
GM 85000

VANDEL

I'LL BE FINE! I FOUND SOME BUSTERS FROM ANOTHER VILLAGE WHO'VE AGREED TO TEAM UP WITH ME.

ALL FIVE OF US ARE LEVEL 20 AND ABOVE. FOR US, THIS ONE WILL BE EASY TO KILL.

I ADMIT YOU'VE GROWN STRONG, BUT... VANDELS ARE NOT THE SAME AS MONSTERS.

PAOLA... LISTEN TO ME. YOU SHOULD GAIN MORE EXPERIENCE BEFORE YOU TRY THE VANDELS.

I KNOW... BUT I CAN'T LEAVE THEM ALONE ANY LONGER.

77

MY DAUGH- TER... ...HAS GONE TO THE BOG OF THE DEAD !!?

IS THAT RIGHT ?

...SHE INSISTED THAT SHE'D BE ABSO- LUTELY FINE.

DESPITE OUR PRO- TESTS...

I KNOW POALA'S GOTTEN VERY STRONG, BUT...

...

SINCE THAT DAY... I'VE COME TO THINK THAT... VANDELS AREN'T SOMETHING HUMANS CAN DEFEAT...

I STILL CAN'T FORGET THAT DAY THREE YEARS AGO.

WE LOST THE ZENON WARRIORS, WHOM WE THOUGHT COULD DEFEAT ANY VANDELS.

I...I SHOULDN'T SAY ANYTHING THAT'D MAKE YOU WORRY... I...

OH... I'M SORRY!

...

...!

CREEAK

TELL ME, AUNTIE!

IS POALA IN DANGER?

WHAT?

CREEAK

79

LOOK!

MUGINE'S BOG OF THE DEAD!!

HE'S CAUSING OUR PONDS AND MARSHES TO ROT.

WE CANNOT LET HIM KEEP DOING AS HE PLEASES.

DON'T WORRY. I'VE ALREADY FOUND A PASSAGE BEHIND THE CASTLE. WE CAN GO THROUGH THAT.

IT'D BE BETTER IF WE COULD PASS THROUGH WITHOUT FIGHTING THEM...

BITING CLAMS AND AQUA DOGS ARE EASY TO DEAL WITH...

...BUT THOSE IRON KNIGHT SHELLS GUARDING THE GATE COULD BE TROUBLE.

WE'LL DIVIDE THE COMMISSION EQUALLY. THAT MEANS WE EXPECT YOU TO WORK JUST AS HARD AS WE DO.

YOU'RE SO PREPARED.

REALLY? I SUPPOSE IT'S WHAT I'D EXPECT FROM THE VETERAN PRIME WARRIORS!

...AND TAKE REVENGE ON BEHALF OF ALL THE VILLAGERS.

RIGHT! I'LL GIVE HIM THE FATAL BLOW...

GRRK

THE FOUR OF US WILL SEAL HIS HANDS AND LEGS, RIGHT?

SO ABOUT OUR PLANS... YOU ALL REMEMBER WHAT TO DO WHEN THE VANDEL SHOWS UP?

SLOSH SLOSH SLOSH

AT THE TOP OF THOSE STAIRS...

RMMRMM

SLOSH

SHAAAA

AHH!

!!!

TAH TAH

HM...
HM...
HM...

TH-THIS PLACE IS GUARDED, TOO!

!!

WELCOME TO MY CASTLE!

TAH

HAH

...A CUTE BUSTER GIRL!

I'LL ENJOY FIGHTING...

YOU'RE... THE VANDEL...

...MUGINE!!

KYAAA

YES... ...I AM MUGINE.

...IT'S TOO LATE TO TURN BACK!!

NEVER MIND...

KII

THIS IS...

WHAT A POWERFUL PRESENCE HE EMANATES...

...A REAL VANDEL!!

SHIVER

YEAH!

EVERYONE! WE'VE GOT NO CHOICE BUT TO FIGHT NOW!!

LET'S FOLLOW THE PLAN!!

YOU'RE TO SEAL THE HANDS AND THE LEGS OF THE VANDEL...

WH- WHAT'RE YOU DOING?!

86

HEH HEH HEH

SO I THOUGHT... WHY NOT TEACH HER A LESSON?

I HEARD THAT A FEMALE BUSTER FROM THE VILLAGE OF ANCKLES HAS BEEN KILLING MY MONSTERS RIGHT AND LEFT.

EVERY-THING WORKED OUT AS I PLANNED!

TH-THIS CAN'T BE...!!

WE'RE JUST FOLLOW-ING THE PLAN!

...IS TO OBTAIN A PART OF THE PERSON!! ALL WE NEED...

SHHLUP

WE DRAW-MASTERS ARE NOT ORDINARY DRAWMEN!

WE CAN COPY EVEN THE ODOR AND PERSONALITY OF THE HUMANS WE IMITATE.

BUT... I DIDN'T SMELL...

!!

KEE HEE HEE HEE!

YOU KILLED THE PRIME WARRIORS!

PLOP

SHHLIP

Y-YOU KILLED THEM!

KEE HEE HEE HEE!

RIIP

SSF

THAT'S EXACTLY WHAT I EXPECTED YOU'D BE.

HUM... 10...20... YOU'RE LEVEL 21!

FLAP

THAT'S WHY IT'S THE LEVEL AT WHICH BUSTERS ARE MOST LIKELY TO LOSE THEIR LIVES!

...WANTING TO DEFEAT STRONGER OPPONENTS AND GET MORE COMMISSIONS.

YOU AGREE?

THAT'S JUST ABOUT WHEN BUSTERS BEGIN TO GET AMBITIOUS...

...!!!

IT'S BECAUSE THEIR HEADS, HANDS AND LEGS ARE SO EASY TO CUT OFF!!

OH... AND DO YOU KNOW WHY THE BUSTERS ARE BRANDED ON THEIR CHESTS?

LET ME DRINK TO THE FEAR IN YOUR EYES!

HA HA HA HA! HOW WONDERFUL!!

SH...

NOW...

CRUNCH CRUNCH CRNCH

RURU

RURURU

RURURU

BA

CLANG

I'VE EXTENDED MY BLACK BOGS TO 84 AREAS, BUT FOOLS CONTINUE TO TRY TO CLEAN THEM UP. YOU'LL SET A GOOD EXAMPLE FOR THEM!

I'LL MAKE SURE YOUR BODY WILL BE RETURNED TO YOUR VILLAGE.

IT'LL HELP YOUR FELLOW HUMANS TO DESPAIR EVEN MORE!!

MWA HA HA!

I WON'T KILL YOU INSTANTLY... PLEASE DIE WITH YOUR FACE DISTORTED IN AS MUCH PAIN AND FEAR AS POSSIBLE.

I UNDER-ESTIMATED HIM! EVEN A TWO-STAR VANDEL... IS TOO MUCH...

N-NO GOOD... THERE'S NOTHING I CAN DO...

GRRRR

BRR BRR

...DAD...

...MOM...

I'M SORRY...

...ONCE I'M A TOP BUSTER, I'LL MARRY YOU!

I PLAN TO BE THE STRONGEST, FIRST-CLASS BUSTER IN THE WORLD.

...BEET...

ONE HUNDRED WOULD BE A GOOD NUMBER OF CUTS...

GYAA

HERE COMES THE VERY FIRST!!

TH-THAT
VOICE...

!!?

WILL
YOU STOP
NOW?

TAK

COULD IT BE?

IT'S BEEN A LONG TIME.

COULD IT REALLY BE?

I'VE GOTTA GET THE WHOLE FAMILY TOGETHER TO MAKE IT AN EXCITING EVENT.

YOU SEE, I'M ABOUT TO GO HOME AND HAVE DINNER WITH HER.

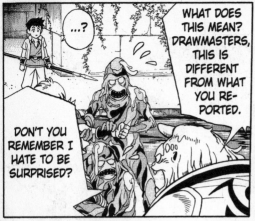

...?

WHAT DOES THIS MEAN? DRAWMASTERS, THIS IS DIFFERENT FROM WHAT YOU RE-PORTED.

DON'T YOU REMEMBER I HATE TO BE SURPRISED?

HE'S NOT PART OF MY PLAN!!

SHE HAS A COMRADE!?

...!?

FIRST OF ALL, WHAT IS HE...

HE'S PROBABLY HER LITTLE BROTHER, JUMPING IN TO SAVE HER WITHOUT THINKING.

HUMPH! ALL RIGHT! THAT MAKES SENSE! *MY PLAN IS STILL GOOD!!*

...BUT UPON CLOSER INSPECTION, IT'S JUST A KID OF LEVEL 11!

MM...I ASSUMED A MUCH STRONGER BUSTER HAD COME TO HELP HER...

L-LEVEL 11...?

TEEHEE HEE

SHOW SOME INITIATIVE AND GET RID OF THIS BOY!!

DRAW-MASTERS!!

HOW-EVER..

DISTURBING MY PERFECT PLAN IS AN EXTREMELY HEAVY CRIME!!

YES, SIR!!

ZOOM ZOOM

...WILL BE INSTANTLY KILLED!!

A LITTLE BOY LIKE HIM...

BEET! RUN AWAY!!

B-BEET...

NO WAY!

...IS THIS TOO EXCITING FOR A GIRL?

HEH HEH...

BA-DOOM

WHO!?

...

99

YOU... KEPT ME WAITING?

...!

YO! SORRY I KEPT YOU WAITING...

...POALA!

WELL... I GUESS I SHOULD AGREE I'M NOT ALL THAT SMART.

IDIOT!

IDIOT!

IDIOT!

IDIOT!

HAVE YOU NOTICED THAT EVERY TIME YOU SEE ME, YOU CALL ME AN IDIOT?

HUH?

YOU KEPT ME WAITING?

DON'T TALK AS IF... AS IF YOU'VE SHOWN UP LATE FOR AN APPOINT-MENT!!

HOW MANY YEARS WERE YOU MISSING?

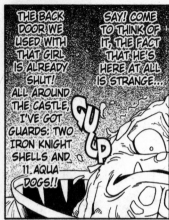

THE BACK DOOR WE USED WITH THAT GIRL IS ALREADY SHUT! ALL AROUND THE CASTLE, I'VE GOT GUARDS: TWO IRON KNIGHT SHELLS AND 11 AQUA DOGS!!

SAY! COME TO THINK OF IT, THE FACT THAT HE'S HERE AT ALL IS STRANGE...

GULP

HE'S ONLY LEVEL 11, BUT HE KILLED FOUR DRAW-MASTERS...INSTANTLY!!

UGH... AAAH... WH-WHAT KIND OF BOY IS HE?

"UNTHINKABLE... IT DOESN'T MAKE SENSE!!

WAAAA

IS THERE AN ENTRANCEWAY OTHER THAN THE GATE?

HOW DID I...?

HOW DID YOU GET IN HERE?

Y-YOU, KID... LET ME ASK YOU A QUESTION...

HUH? LEVEL 11...?

YOU'RE JUST LEVEL 11!

D-DON'T TELL ME THINGS THAT DON'T MAKE SENSE!!

YOU MEAN YOU SNUCK IN PAST THE GUARDS?

THE GUARDS? IF YOU'RE TALKING ABOUT THE IRON KNIGHT SHELLS, I TOOK CARE OF THEM.

AH!

LOOK OVER THERE!

WHATEVER YOU SAY... I THREW THEM TO YOU JUST A WHILE BACK.

OF COURSE! THAT FIRST PUNCH FROM THE IRON KNIGHT SHELLS SCRATCHED ME A LITTLE THERE...

A KID LIKE YOU COULD NEVER DEFEAT THEM.

THE IRON KNIGHT SHELLS ARE MY STRONGEST SUBORDINATES.

MY... MY IRON KNIGHT SHELLS...!!

GLUB

103

THERE MUST BE SOMETHING I CAN STILL DO... SOME WAY TO GET BACK ON THE PLAN!

RIP

RRIIIP

CALM DOWN...

CALM DOWN...

THUD

MY HAND-MADE SPEAR!

GEEZ!

SHING SHING

BEET!!

TADOOM

GYA HA HA... NOW YOU'VE GOT NO WEAPON...

EVEN THOUGH YOU'RE STRONGER THAN I THOUGHT, YOU CAN'T DO MUCH NOW...

106

YOU KNOW, I HAD HIGH HOPES...

...BUT YOU'RE PRETTY LAME, AREN'T YOU?

BUT YOU... YOU PLOT A SURPRISE ATTACK AND SEND OUT YOUR MONSTERS WHEN THE SITUATION TURNS BAD. THERE'RE NO VANDELS LIKE THAT AMONG THE STRONG ONES.

THERE ARE A LOT OF STRONG VANDELS WITH ONLY TWO STARS, BUT THEY USUALLY COME RIGHT OUT FRONT TO FIGHT.

A BEGINNER LIKE YOU SHOULDN'T TALK LIKE THE VETERANS!!!

ACCORDING TO MY EXPERIENCE, THAT IS.

...A MOUND OF WORK AHEAD OF ME!!

I'VE GOT...

SWAAAA

...GUYS?

ISN'T THAT RIGHT...

WHII!!

SHI!!

G-CAN IT...

...POSSIBLY BE!?

THE PROOF OF THE STRONGEST BUSTERS...

...THE SAIGA?

BEET... YOU CAN USE IT?

OOO

I TOLD YOU BEFORE.

THE BIG JOB...?

YUP! IF I COULDN'T USE THIS, I WOULDN'T BE EVENLY MATCHED AGAINST VANDELS. WITHOUT IT, I WON'T BE ABLE TO TAKE ON THE BIG JOB!

I'M GONNA END IT WITH MY HANDS!!

THIS DARK AGE!

Chapter 3:
The Time of Departure!

CRE AK

REALLY?

DID HE REALLY COME BACK?

YES!

TAK TAK

Z...

ZENON...!?

118

GOOSH GOOSH

...BEET...

LONG TIME NO SEE!

YO, UNCLE!

THANKS.

BEET!

YOU LOOK GREAT!

FALLING ASLEEP IN FRONT OF EVERYONE IS SUPPOSED TO BE MY SPECIALTY, THOUGH...

HEH

WHAT? POALA...

SHE FELL ASLEEP FROM FATIGUE...

WE WERE ALL WORRIED ABOUT YOU. BEET, YOU'VE GOT TO WRITE EVERY NOW AND THEN...

THIS PAST THREE YEARS... WITHOUT ANY WORD FROM YOU... SHE WAS WORRIED ABOUT YOU MORE THAN ANYONE ELSE.

SHE MUST'VE FELT RELIEVED AFTER SEEING YOUR FACE, BEET.

UNCLE, WHAT'S WRONG...

...WITH YOUR ARM?

!!

OU-OUCH...

BECAUSE OF MUGINE'S BOG OF THE DEAD, OUR VILLAGE IS LOADED WITH COUNTLESS BLACK BOGS...

AND ALL THE BOGS ARE INHABITED BY MUD LIZARDS.

IF YOU'RE BITTEN, THIS IS WHAT HAPPENS!

OH... THIS...

THE MEDICINE WE NEED HAS COST US A LOT...

HE'S GOTTEN A LOT BETTER THAN BEFORE, THOUGH. FIRST YEAR, HE COULDN'T MOVE HIS ARM AT ALL.

THAT'S WHAT SHE SAID...

...AND SHE BECAME A BUSTER.

I CAN ALSO EARN SOME MONEY. THAT WAY, I CAN KILL TWO BIRDS WITH ONE STONE, DON'T YOU THINK?

I'LL BECOME A BUSTER. ONCE I'M A BUSTER, I'LL TAKE REVENGE ON OUR ENEMIES!

...

SHE'S BEEN THROUGH A LOT...

I HAD NO IDEA.

SO THAT'S WHAT HAPPENED...

°°°°°°

IS IT OKAY FOR ME TO USE THEM?

I HAVE SOME IN THE SHED...

DO YOU HAVE SOME EXTRA SPEARS?

UNCLE...

SURE.

THUNK

IT'S NOT A PROBLEM, BUT...

I'LL BE BACK IN A BIT.

LET HER SLEEP.

SHFF

122

THAT MIGHT BE THE CASE, BUT...

REMEMBER, I'M THE MAN WHO CAN FIGHT THREE DAYS AND NIGHTS!

I SLEPT ALL DAY YESTERDAY, SO I'M TOTALLY FINE.

WHERE'RE YOU GOING THIS LATE, ANYWAY?

THAT'S RIGHT.

YOU'D BETTER REST YOUR-SELF...

YOU FOUGHT WITH HER, RIGHT?

WHILE YOU'RE ALL SLEEPING, I'LL MAKE TOMORROW A BETTER DAY!

I'M OKAY!

CLICK

...?

...!

WH–
WH–

WHAT'RE THESE!?

HUBBUB

WHOAAA!!

HUBBUB

CHUCK

LOOK AT THAT!

OH, POALA!

WHAT'S WRONG, EVERYONE!?

SHAA

MUTTER

BABBLE

BABBLE BABBLE

!!?

IT'S... BEET...!!

WHO COULD HAVE DONE SUCH A DEED?

...

ALL THE BLACK BOGS HAVE DISAPPEARED FROM THE VILLAGE OVERNIGHT!!

I DON'T UNDERSTAND WHY HE'S SO STRONG AT ONLY LEVEL 11... BUT BEET'S REALLY GOOD!!

IT'S INCREDIBLE!!

INCREDIBLE!

!!

NO MATTER WHAT KIND OF VANDELS SHOW UP, WE'LL BE OKAY...

...NOW THAT BEET'S HERE!!

127

OH, POALA! YOU'RE UP.

!?

BEET!!

AND...

YOU BROUGHT IT FOR ME, THANKS.

AH!

THANKS FOR YOUR JACKET!

I MIGHT NOT BE ABLE TO CARRY THEM ALL BY MY-SELF...

TO THE APPRAIS-ER'S HOUSE!

IT'S PERFECT TIMING! WILL YOU COME WITH ME?

HUH?

THE APPRAI-SER'S HOUSE?

I GOT MY COMMISSION SETTLED!

THREE YEARS' WORTH, YOU KNOW...

WH- WHAT'S THIS!?

THAT OLD LADY AT THE APPRAISER'S HOUSE THREW A FIT. SHE SCANNED MY EYES TO MAKE SURE I WAS TELLING THE TRUTH.

NOW MY EYE- BALLS ARE PRICKLING...

TH-THREE YEARS WORTH... !!?

BECAUSE VISITING THE APPRAISER STINKS!

WHAT?

BUT WHY DID YOU ACCUMULATE SO MUCH?

YIPES!

WHEN I THOUGHT ABOUT IT YESTERDAY, I REALIZED I MUST'VE ACCUMULATED A LOT OF MONEY, SINCE I'VE DEFEATED SOME OF THE VANDELS...

HA HA

IT WAS FUN TO GET BRANDED, UNTIL ABOUT LEVEL 10. THEN IT BECAME A CHORE. I JUST BRUSHED IT OFF.

NO WONDER. I THOUGHT YOU WERE TOO STRONG TO BE LEVEL 11!

HOW MISLEADING...

BUT I WAS SHOCKED AT THE APPRAISER'S HOUSE. I'M ALREADY LEVEL 28!

HA HA... BEET'S ALWAYS BEEN DIFFERENT FROM COMMON FOLK. HE'S ON A WHOLE OTHER SCALE!

...ONLY YOU COULD BE THAT, BEET!

A STUPID BUST- ER...

WHAM

GEEZ...

IS IT REALLY?

HEE HEE

A HA HA HA

IT'S JUST LIKE BEET.

⁉

?

ALL RIGHT! IT'S ABOUT TIME I GET GOING!

NOW THAT THE VILLAGE'S SWAMPS ARE ALL CLEANED UP... PLEASE USE THE MONEY TO PAY FOR UNCLE'S TREATMENTS AND HIRE SOME BUSTERS.

131

 TO GET STRONGER THAN I AM NOW, I MUST GO FURTHER, A LOT FURTHER OUT THERE.

FOR THREE YEARS, I'VE TRAINED MYSELF OUTSIDE THE VILLAGE, BUT NOW I NEED TO GO AFTER THE REAL THING.

GET GOING? TO WHERE...?

I PROBABLY WON'T COME BACK UNTIL I GET RID OF THEM ALL.

IN THE WORLD, THERE'RE LOADS OF EXTRAORDINARILY STRONG VANDELS. THEY'RE THE ONES WHO HAVE BROUGHT DARKNESS TO OUR WORLD...

I STOPPED BY... TO TELL YOU THAT.

132

THAT'S TRUE... HOW MANY TIMES HAVE I HEARD YOU SAY, "I'M GONNA BE THE WORLD'S STRONGEST BUSTER"?

YOU'VE NEVER LISTENED ONCE YOU'VE MADE UP YOUR MIND.

I SUPPOSE WE CAN'T STOP YOU...

...FOR THIS IS YOUR HOME.

THAT'S RIGHT... YOU CAN SHOW YOUR FACE HERE ANYTIME...

I'M SURE THIS WON'T BE OUR LAST MEETING.

BEST OF LUCK!

GRP

BANG

WHAT THE HECK ARE YOU SAYING?

133

BEET, ARE YOU SERIOUS WHEN YOU SAY THAT?

END THE DARK AGE?

BOTH MOM AND DAD... BELIEVING THE WORDS THAT COME OUT OF THIS IDIOT'S MOUTH!!

YOU'RE PLAYING GAMES, WHILE THE REST OF US ARE STRUGGLING TO SURVIVE!

I CAN'T BELIEVE IT! "BUSTER OF JUSTICE," HUH? IT'S NOT LOGICAL. IT SOUNDS LIKE A CHILDISH FAIRY TALE.

I'VE ALWAYS BEEN SERIOUS ABOUT IT...

...POALA.

...!

ooo

YOU MIGHT BE A LITTLE STRONGER NOW, BUT YOU'RE TOTALLY OUT OF LINE.

I THOUGHT... YOU'D RETURNED TO PROTECT OUR VILLAGE WITH ME!

POALA... THERE USED TO BE BUSTERS WHO FOUGHT FOR MORE THAN THEIR OWN LIVES, WEREN'T THERE?

HERE...

...AT THIS TABLE...

TAP

...THE FIVE OF THEM SAT HERE.

135

THE ZENON
WARRIORS...
!!

IT'S NOT LOGIC THAT MAKES ME WANT TO BE LIKE THEM.

THANKS TO THEM, I CAN BELIEVE IN JUSTICE.

BEET...

THAT'S WHY I WANNA BE AS STRONG AS THE FIVE OF THEM COMBINED AND BECOME THE BUSTER OF JUSTICE!

...

BESIDES, ALL FIVE OF THEM GAVE ME THEIR LIVES.

DAH DAH

POALA !!

...YOU IDIOT!!!

...

137

OPEN UP!

IF SO, IT'S NO PROBLEM.

STOP, BEET!

A VANDEL IS WAITING OUT THERE.

A VANDEL...

GROOOOWN...

ALL RIGHT, THEN...

JUST BE CAREFUL.

GRM GRM

GRM GRM

GRM

YOU MEAN SOME FAT HUNK OF MUD?

140

...SO I KNEW YOU WEREN'T DEAD.

GRANNY AT THE APPRAISER'S HOUSE DIDN'T GIVE ME THE COMMISSION ON YOU...

SHA

NOW I DON'T HAVE TO LOOK FOR YOU.

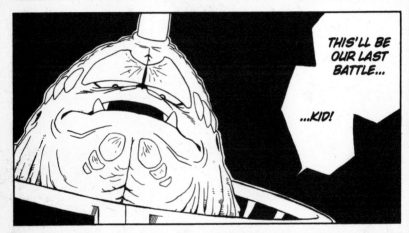

THIS'LL BE OUR LAST BATTLE...

...KID!

!!?

BUT I'M SURPRISED YOU'RE FACING ME STRAIGHT ON.

GIVES ME SOME RESPECT FOR YOU.

IF YOU'RE AROUND, NO MATTER HOW MUCH I CLEAN UP THE VILLAGE, YOU'LL CONTAMINATE IT AGAIN!

OF COURSE.

SHA

UGH...
UGH...

GWB

GWB

GWB

GWB

UGGH...

GWB

OOF
OOF

I NEEDED 4 DRAW-MASTERS, 5 IRON KNIGHT SHELLS AND 9 AQUA DOGS...

IT WAS A LOT OF WORK TO REGENERATE THE HALF OF MY BODY YOU SLICED OFF...

GOBBLING UP YOUR SUB-ORDINATES JUST SO YOU CAN REGENERATE YOUR-SELF!

WHAT A HOR-RIBLE THING TO DO...

FORGET WHAT I JUST SAID.

I ACKNOWLEDGE THAT WITHOUT RESERVATION! YOU'RE STRONG...

IT'S INTERESTING THAT YOUR SAIGA IS THAT POWERFUL.

HOO HOO

BUT THAT'S FINE.

WHERE'D HIS RIGHT ARM GO?

THAT'S WEIRD...

...WILL BE TERMINATED!!

I'LL MAKE SURE YOUR EXISTENCE...

KRAAA

KRMM

HOWEVER, I'VE GOT THE PRIDE OF A VANDEL, AFTER ALL...

143

144

HEH HEH HEH

EVEN IF YOUR SAIGA'S STRONG, YOU PROBABLY CAN'T USE IT WITHOUT YOUR HANDS, RIGHT?

C'MON...

UGH UGH UGH

OO-OOPS!!

...!!

GRUM

RUM RUM

SHU

RUM RUM

!!?

JUST AS I PLANNED!

145

NOT WITH THIS CRAP!

CUT ME?

OOF

ARGH OOF

TUMP

KYAAH!

GIVE UP. IT'S USELESS!

FORCE WON'T WORK AGAINST IT!

SQUEE SQUEE

I'LL RIP IT TO SHREDS!

ARRRGH

WHOOOSH

BESIDES, IF YOU WIGGLE LIKE THAT...

GRAAAAR

POALA!!

MY DIVINE ATTACK...

YOU'RE THE ONE WHO'LL DIE!

HAVE YOU COME TO DIE OR WHAT?

THAT GIRL!!

151

152

160

HE'S ABSOLUTELY DIFFERENT FROM ANY OF THE ORDINARY BUSTERS!!

HE'S DIFFERENT!

HMMM...

CHK

I THINK... BEET WAS...

161

THANKS, POA—

IT WAS CLOSE. I ALMOST GOT KILLED...

VOO OOM

WHOOSH

ER—

IT'S—

OU-OU-OUCH!!

GYAAH

ooo

YOU SAID THERE ARE LOADS OF STRONGER VANDELS FARTHER OUT IN THE WORLD... SO WHY ARE YOU ALMOST KILLED THE MOMENT YOU'VE LEFT THE VILLAGE?

WHAT'S THE MATTER...

...WITH YOU!?

YOU'LL GO EVEN IF I TRY TO STOP YOU, RIGHT?

FINE! GO WHEREVER YOUR HEART DESIRES!

BUT...

THAT'S—

THE WAY THINGS STAND, YOU'RE GOING OUT TO DIE ALONE!!

HOW CAN YOU SAY THAT YOU'LL END THE DARK AGE?

WHAT!?

I'M COMING WITH YOU!

POALA... YOU...

THE NUMBER TWO...?

I'M THE NO. 2 OF THE BEET WARRIORS!!

MY PARENTS ARE OKAY WITH IT!

LOOK!

164

BESIDES, DAD SAYS THAT HAVING YOU OUT THERE ALONE, WANDERING AROUND WITH NO COMMON SENSE, WILL WORRY HIM AND MAKE HIS ARM SWELL UP!

EVEN IF I'M NOT AROUND, WITH THE MONEY YOU'VE GIVEN THEM, THEY'LL BE FINE FOR A WHILE...

ooo

ALL RIGHT!

LET'S GO!

IF I HADN'T COME TO HELP, YOU WOULD'VE BEEN KILLED BY MUGINE A MOMENT AGO.

YOU SHOULD WORRY ABOUT YOURSELF FIRST!

I DON'T EVEN KNOW HOW MANY YEARS IT'LL TAKE!!

ARE YOU SERIOUS, POALA!? I'LL BE FIGHTING LOADS OF VANDELS...

WHAT WOULD YOU DO WITHOUT ME? YOU, SOMEONE WITH NO PLAN AND NO UNDERSTANDING OF MONEY... AN IDIOT... LIKE YOU... ALL ALONE?

...?

I'VE ALREADY MADE UP MY MIND!

AH, WELL...

IT'S NOT LOGIC...

...THAT MAKES ME WANT TO COME!!

OH WELL! "BEET WARRIORS" SOUNDS PRETTY GOOD!

HEH HEH...

I CAN'T ARGUE WITH THAT, CAN I?

...HA HA.

166

BEET... YOU KNOW, JUST BEING NEAR YOU...

...YUP... IT'S NOT BAD...

...THE WAY I FEEL RIGHT NOW.

...I THINK I CAN BELIEVE IN JUSTICE!!

167

BEET THE WORLD

THE WORLD OF
BEET the VANDEL BUSTER • PART 1

Let's look at the exotic and expansive world of "Beet." Here we'll analyze it in its entirety. Listed in this section are the main figures of the Dark Age...

The Vandels are humanity's greatest threat. Vandels create monsters in the blink of an eye, devastating the earth and forcing humans to live in fear. People have come to call the endless, hellish era created by the Vandels the "Dark Age," and they regret living in such a terrible reality. In an attempt to break this vicious cycle, a new occupation has been born: the Vandel Busters, warriors dedicated to conquering the Vandels. At first they were simply bounty hunters, but now the system for Vandel Busters is formally established with supporting nations and organizations. Vandel Busters are usually called Busters for short. They each have unique battle skills, and they live off of the commissions they earn by killing Vandels and monsters.

- - - - - - - - - - - - - - - - - - - -

▲ Warrior groups all over the world are fighting against Vandels.

Anyone can become a Buster without having any specific qualifications. All one needs to do is sign a contract. However, only a few Busters become powerful enough to actually defeat Vandels. Large commissions are promised to those who kill Vandels, and many strong Busters dream of becoming rich overnight, but most of them end up dead. It is, indeed, a very risky occupation.

THEY ARE THE DARK AND DIRTY PROFESSIONALS WHO HUNT DOWN EVIL!

BEET THE WORLD

BASIC GEAR OF A BUSTER

SAIGA

This is the ultimate weapon. Only the most capable Buster can learn to use it. It's the last weapon a Buster resorts to in battle. See the next page for more details.

THESE ARE THE MARKS OF A DEMON-HUNTING WARRIOR!

BUSTER'S JACKET

When a Buster reaches Level 10, he or she receives this jacket from the Appraiser's House. It's a sort of uniform for Busters.

BRANDING

This brand, the proof of a Buster's occupation, is stamped on his or her chest when the contract is made. The symbol uses an ancient number system. When a Buster's level rises, he or she is branded with a higher number.

Beet ▶ is currently Level 28.

UNDER JACKET

The clothing a Buster wears under the Buster's Jacket is called the Under Jacket. Although inferior to the Buster's Jacket, the Under Jacket is still relatively strong protective gear, and it's flexible, making it perfect for all kinds of actions. There are various types of Under Jackets made to match each Buster's fighting style.

WEAPON

Usually, Busters choose whatever weapons they prefer to fight against Vandels and monsters. Beet uses his handmade spears, while Poala uses two daggers.

ISN'T THAT RIGHT...

...GUYS?

The powerful magic Vandels use is called the Dark Power, and it is known to tap evil energy from the depths below ground. The counterpart, which humans use, is a superhuman force called "Divine Power." Divine Power taps the energy within the atmosphere. The power from the atmosphere is transformed into fire and ice, enabling the Divine Attack. When the Divine Power reaches its extremity, it allows the energy of the atmosphere to produce a physical substance. This is the power a Buster uses as his or her last resort: the Saiga. A Saiga is the ultimate weapon of a Buster, allowing him or her to attack with overwhelming Divine Power, inflicting fatal damage to Vandels, despite their powerful bodies.

THIS IS THE STRONGEST PROOF OF A BUSTER. IT'S AN ULTIMATE WEAPON HIDDEN WITHIN HIS OR HER BODY.

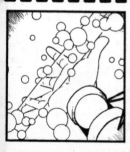

▲ An enormous amount of Divine Power is required to materialize a Saiga.

Saiga do not usually exist in the atmosphere. Instead, during a battle, a Saiga is brought out of a Buster's chest in the form of a glowing ball of light before it changes into its physical form. The Buster's body channels and materializes the elements in the atmosphere. Using the Divine Power, a Buster creates an ideal weapon that he or she has visualized in his or her mind. Beet received five Saiga from the Zenon Warriors, which still exist as glowing balls of energy inside Beet's body.

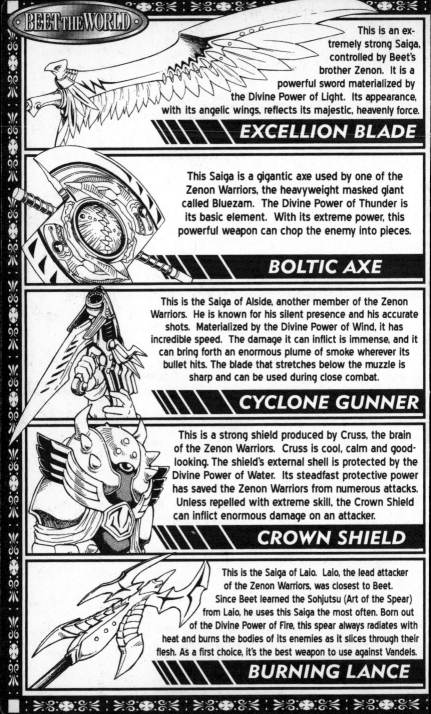

This is an extremely strong Saiga, controlled by Beet's brother Zenon. It is a powerful sword materialized by the Divine Power of Light. Its appearance, with its angelic wings, reflects its majestic, heavenly force.

EXCELLION BLADE

This Saiga is a gigantic axe used by one of the Zenon Warriors, the heavyweight masked giant called Bluezam. The Divine Power of Thunder is its basic element. With its extreme power, this powerful weapon can chop the enemy into pieces.

BOLTIC AXE

This is the Saiga of Alside, another member of the Zenon Warriors. He is known for his silent presence and his accurate shots. Materialized by the Divine Power of Wind, it has incredible speed. The damage it can inflict is immense, and it can bring forth an enormous plume of smoke wherever its bullet hits. The blade that stretches below the muzzle is sharp and can be used during close combat.

CYCLONE GUNNER

This is a strong shield produced by Cruss, the brain of the Zenon Warriors. Cruss is cool, calm and good-looking. The shield's external shell is protected by the Divine Power of Water. Its steadfast protective power has saved the Zenon Warriors from numerous attacks. Unless repelled with extreme skill, the Crown Shield can inflict enormous damage on an attacker.

CROWN SHIELD

This is the Saiga of Laio. Laio, the lead attacker of the Zenon Warriors, was closest to Beet. Since Beet learned the Sohjutsu (Art of the Spear) from Laio, he uses this Saiga the most often. Born out of the Divine Power of Fire, this spear always radiates with heat and burns the bodies of its enemies as it slices through their flesh. As a first choice, it's the best weapon to use against Vandels.

BURNING LANCE

The Appraiser's House is the base of activities for the Busters. The Association of Busters has established Appraiser's Houses all over the world. The Association pays out commissions to subjugate Vandels and the overflowing number of monsters. The amount of commission the Association pays out is based on the strength of the opponent. At the house, the managing appraiser acknowledges the work done, pays out the commission, and approves an increase in level.

In addition, the Appraiser's House is an effective place to gather information. Busters can learn the price of various Vandels, as well as available jobs from nearby towns and villages. Most of the appraisers are old men or old women, but they're all experienced Busters and are expert Divine Attackers. Unsuspecting intruders can be easily beaten away.

APPRAISER'S HOUSE

THIS IS THE BASE FOR THE VANDEL BUSTERS' ACTIVITY!

RETINAL APPRAISAL

This is a special way of appraising Busters using Divine Power. Appraisers examine a Buster's eyes and verify the images of enemies' deaths imprinted on the Buster's retina. Once the deaths are ascertained, the Buster is entitled to the commission and promotion points. If the death of the enemy is in doubt, the Buster is denied the commission. This is the standard and only method of evaluating the work of Busters throughout the world, and a Buster can go from one Appraiser's House to the next without disturbing his or her record.

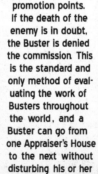

▲ Because the last appraiser's face is imprinted in the Buster's retina, the Buster cannot be paid twice for a completed job.

▼ For Busters, the brand works as an I.D.

In accordance with standardized scoring, Busters accumulate promotion points as they get rid of Vandels and monsters, and Busters' levels are upped accordingly by an appraiser. Busters' levels are clearly marked on their chests. The process is called Branding. Busters are pressed with hot iron, and ancient numbers are burnt onto their chests. The ancient numbers look somewhat similar to Roman numerals. Each line represents one point. With just a glance, a Buster's level is easily known by anyone.

LEVEL UP

◄ Busters insist that the branding does not hurt much.

WANTED NOTICE

On the wall of the Appraiser's House, there are usually numerous Wanted Notices. The most important type is the notice relating to Vandels. Basic information, such as the place where the Vandel is based, the number of his stars, and the amount of commission, is written on the notice. Multiple of copies are readily available, and Busters can take as many copies as they want. The moment a Vandel is dead, a notice for that Vandel is eliminated from every Appraiser's House around the world.

MG

In this world, all money is in coin form. The basic denomination is the MG, or Maggie. The lowest value of a coin is 1 MG. There are numerous coins, from 1MG coins to 10,000MG coins, and, depending on the total amount of money, various combinations of coins can be used. An Appraiser's House typically contains huge sums of MG, but the appraiser of the hut is the only one who knows where the money is hidden.

▶ Beltorze -- a five-star Vandel with overwhelming powers.
He is also known as the King of Tragedy.

▼ Mugine -- a Vandel with numerous abilities who lives in the Bog of the Dead. Although he's only a two-star Vandel, he's not easy to defeat.

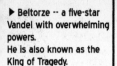

The natural enemies of humans, Vandels are the strongest and the most terrible beings in the world. Their fighting power is tremendous, their vitality is unlimited, and it is not too much to state that they're physically the most perfect creatures that have ever lived. They are the reason behind the Dark Age, this long era of struggle that humans face. Some go about inflicting violence around the world, while others produce armies of monsters, causing disorder in human society. They're truly evil.

- -

A common characteristic of the Vandels is the tremendous power they use, called Dark Power. When Dark Power is transformed into aggressive energy for an attack, it is called a Dark Attack. Another common characteristic is their immense physical power, which ranges from ten to one hundred times that of ordinary human beings. But the strongest bond all Vandels share is the pleasure they feel in annihilating humans and destroying the world.
In accordance with their standard of distinction, jewels called "stars" are embedded in their left arms. The number of stars determines their status. Naturally, the more stars a Vandel has, the stronger he is. Therefore, stars can be used to figure out the strength of each Vandel, and humans are well aware of their meaning.

VANDELS & MONSTERS

THEY ARE THE MAIN PLAYERS OF THE DARK AGE. THEY ARE THE FORCE OF DARKNESS THAT DEVASTATES THE EARTH.

DRAWMASTER
Stronger version of a Drawman. It has a powerful talent for mimicry.

IRON KNIGHT SHELL
Covered in a tough shell, it belongs to the strongest class of shellfish monsters.

Vandels create numerous monsters as their subordinates, and some of them are as strong as the Vandels themselves. Some understand language, work as partners, and can serve as the Vandels' personal guards. Busters must deal with these types of monsters carefully.

UPPER CLASS MONSTERS

AQUA DOG
A monster whose body is made of water. It is a competent guard dog.

DRAWMAN
This shape-shifting monster infiltrates villages by impersonating a villager.

These are what ordinary humans refer to as monsters. They have moderately high intelligence and are able to make decisions. They are well suited as opponents for trained Busters, but common people are no match for their strength. They are strong opponents and should not be engaged without a determined focus.

MIDDLE CLASS MONSTERS

CANNECK
It likes to eat coins and is troublesome.

BITING CLAM
The first monster Beet defeated. It has a strong set of teeth.

These are vicious creatures resembling animals or insects. They don't take direct orders from Vandels. Once released, they reproduce and attack uncontrollably, inflicting massive damage on the human world. They're not very strong, but they should not be overlooked.

LOWER CLASS MONSTER

Coming Next Volume

Beltorze is back and more powerful than ever—the strongest Vandel of all. And after shopping for some new monster minions at the Dark House of Sorcery you can bet that he's out to cause more trouble! Meanwhile, Beet and Poala have to duke it out with another powerful Vandel, Grineed. But he's just the beginning of their troubles...

Available Now!